Burn Your Budget

How to Spend Your Way to Financial Freedom

Wendy Brookhouse

Burn Your Budget

Printed by:
90-Minute Books
302 Martinique Drive
Winter Haven, FL 33884
www.90minutebooks.com

Copyright © 2016, Wendy Brookhouse

Published in the United States of America

ISBN-13: 978-1945733222
ISBN-10: 1945733225

For more information on 90-Minute Books including finding out how you can
publish your own lead generating book, visit www.90minutebooks.com or call
(863) 318-0464

Here's What's Inside…

Introduction

Whether you make a lot of money or not, whether you're a spender or a saver, there's always that question: "How much can I spend and still achieve my goals?"

There is a way to fully enjoy your life today without having to sacrifice your future.

I came into the financial industry differently than most people. Because of that I never had any restrictions put on me as to how I could work with or help my clients. As a result, I've been able to be innovative in my approach and to develop ways to accommodate my clients' natural behavior when it comes to their finances.

I strongly believe that money isn't just about the math. It's also about all the things that are going on in your life and how you're feeling about them; these aspects often affect what you do and how you spend.

One of my first financial plans, crafted over a decade ago, was for a friend who took her shopping pretty seriously. I had to come up with a plan that accommodated her natural tendencies but gave her some boundaries, which no one had helped her create before. I ensured her *One Number Solution*™ included money to spend on her shopping habit because cutting her off wouldn't have been sustainable for her. This gave her something to focus on, and rather than resisting, she really enjoyed living the plan.

What I cover in this book isn't being taught in schools. You are taught a lot of things in school, but practical things like how to align your spending with your goals, how credit works and how to distinguish between the price and the cost of something, aren't among those lessons.

What follows is an interview style approach, highlighting some of the frequently asked questions about the *One Number Solution*

To Your Success!

Wendy Brookhouse

Who Is It For?

Jonathan: Good afternoon. I'm excited to be here with Wendy Brookhouse. Wendy is going to share with us her thoughts and ideas on how to spend your way to financial freedom. Welcome, Wendy.

Wendy: Thank you.

Jonathan: You have given your book a really provocative title. Do you really believe that people can spend their way to financial freedom?

Wendy: I do! I believe that with the right easy-to-manage system, where their spending plan is in alignment with their goals and dreams, people can spend their way to financial freedom.

Jonathan: What is financial freedom? Is it being debt free? Having lots of savings?

Wendy: Interesting questions…which have a multitude of answers. Financial freedom is deeply personal and different for everyone. For some it does mean getting their unwanted debt paid off, while for others it means that they can take a major trip every year. When putting a plan together we always take the time up front to understand what is important to the individual and then prioritize those goals.

Jonathan: Who is the *One Number Solution™* for?

Wendy: It would be very easy to assume that this type of planning is only for people who don't have a lot money or who have a lot of debt.

This kind of planning does work in those situations, but it really shines when it is done with people who have cash flow or access to capital. People who earn good money can be just as stressed about finances as those without.

The *One Number Solution*™ is for people who have guilt and anxiety around money.

It's for people who want to communicate better with their partner about money.

It's for people who want a system to help figure out if a purchase is worth it.

It's for people who want to understand what happens to their overall plan when they have a major financial decision to make.

It's for people who not only want to know what to do, but more importantly *how* to do it.

The Budget Is Dead

Jonathan: What do people need to know about how to spend their way to financial freedom?

Wendy: Budgets don't work. They are too complicated and too rigid to be sustainable in real world practice.

There are so many things to track and remember. Thinking, "I spent this much on groceries, this much on gas, this much on clothing…So how much do I have left to spend in each category tomorrow or next week?" becomes very convoluted.

In *Your Brain at Work* by David Rock he discusses how your brain can only really handle one thing at a time. Multitasking is an illusion. We have so many competing priorities in our lives which want our attention – family, friends, career and other passions. Once you add in your financial life it can become very overwhelming and you burn out trying to remember everything you're supposed to track.

Sometimes I think the ways in which the world has tried to help us with technology have just added a layer of complexity. A number of banks have developed software programs and tracking systems that categorize everything you buy. They then show you what you have done, and you can compare it to what you meant to do.

The problem with these plans is that they are an "after the spending" kind of thing.

You're still trying to track different categories and unless you are constantly monitoring them, it becomes a measure of what you have done and not a tool to know if you can spend or not. As humans, we need an early warning system.

Alternatively, there are all kinds of envelopes and jars that people use. Those are cash systems, and they seem to work a little bit better because they're ahead of the curve in terms of the actual spending. You know where you are with your money at any point. As systems go, they are more proactive, but still require effort to maintain and track.

Jonathan: How does the *One Number Solution*™ differ from these other systems?

Wendy: There are no categories to keep track of. There are no calculations to make. There is only one number, unique to you and your financial situation that you need to pay attention to. All you have to do is keep that number in the black for seven days and you're successful!

To arrive at that one number, our team breaks everything down into annual, monthly and weekly spending. We integrate all of your must-haves and ensure they are met and automated in your plan.

Once that is completed, we come up with a weekly cash amount, your *One Number Solution*™, and we ask you to spend within that number for the week.

Every seven days, you take out that same amount in cash and spend it on your discretionary or more emotional purchases for the week. Having only one number to think about is what really reduces the worry.

You know immediately if you're on-plan or off-plan. We look at it as the fence that you can build around your own behavior. If you crawl over the fence and spend using your credit card for something you should have used your cash for, you know that you're off-plan. This can also be a great catalyst for conversation about priorities – was the reason you climbed the fence worth it?

Jonathan: What is the biggest benefit of the *One Number Solution™*?

Wendy: The biggest advantage is the reduction of stress and anxiety around money, and of course how simple yet dynamic the system is.

We've discovered that the plan gives people a variety of great results. In addition to reducing stress, they have a detailed guide for how to implement their spending and a system to determine if particular purchases are worth it.

They're actually able to look at the purchases in the context of the overall plan and say, "Yes, I do think it's okay that I take an extra year to pay off my debt so I can purchase this particular item, go on this vacation, etc."

It allows them to make informed decisions and to simplify their financial life down to that one number, which makes it so much easier for them to follow.

When I think of a typical budget, it involves a phenomenal amount of "mental accounting". People have to remember how much has been spent or what is left in each category. Many people fit it all into an elaborate spreadsheet, and sometimes they even go so far as to color-code their work!

Once they have these beautiful spreadsheets all done, the hard work actually starts. Budgets mean that they have to think of everything. They have to track, mark things down, and remember what they did.

But life isn't usually that cut and dried. When we budget, we set a target amount over a period of time. For example, let's say we decided to spend $200 a week on groceries. One week every kind of household soap runs out (and they seem to have an uncanny ability to do it all in the same week!) That week you have to spend an extra $50 on dish soap, laundry soap, shampoo, etc. You tell yourself that you'll only spend $150 the next week. In an ideal world that would be what happens, but in my experience it rarely does.

We've found that simplifying your weekly spending to one number and working within that number makes it much easier for people. That way, they don't have to accurately recall and track everything, and they can make adjustments within their one number based on what is actually happening in their lives.

What Are You Doing Now?

Jonathan: Okay, so the budget is dead! What process do you follow to develop your *One Number Solution™*?

Wendy: As I mentioned, financial freedom is deeply personal. A plan only works if it begins with your goals and dreams. We take the time to really quantify what success looks like for each client.

Once we've established what the end results need to be, we go back to analyze and evaluate their *current* spending.

It's amazing how someone's spending rarely corresponds with the budget spreadsheets they provide. What I find fascinating is that their budget will say that they should have $1,000 left each month, but when I ask, "How much do you have in your bank account right now?" it never matches!!

Often, it's because there's a lot of unconscious spending going on. They're not aware of where their money is going or if it's going where they meant it to go. We've put a name to that: Missing Money Syndrome™. Where is that money they thought they were going to have? It's just gone.

So the next step of the process is called Reality Data™, where we analyze three months of their actual spending to see what is really happening, and identify the traps where that Missing Money goes.

It's not about judgement, but rather a chance for the client to see how they manage and spend their money now.

The Reality Data™ has two major sections: Discretionary versus Non-Discretionary spends. Non-discretionary covers things like mortgage, car, debt and utility payments. Those we calculate and build into the plan.

The Discretionary is where we can start to see some really interesting patterns. We look for spends in places that we know are traps for that Missing Money, places like Costco and drugstores where you spend more than you intend to.

We break down spending between convenience food and restaurants. We look at the frequency of how many times you made purchases in those categories over the course of a month. Then we look at the average amount spent because it's the little things, the few dollars here and the $10 there, which kill people's plans more so than the big purchases. People tend to be more conscious of the big purchases than the cumulative effect of the little ones.

We don't feel that it is our place to judge where the money was spent, but rather show the totals, the frequency of spending and the average. If you meant to spend $300 on convenience foods and beverages, that is fine. If you didn't know it added up to that, now you do and can make a change if you want to. This process brings the unconscious spending into the conscious and is an important part of creating a successful plan.

Jonathan: Is there something subliminal about your plan?

Wendy: At some level, it is the exact opposite. As one of my clients recently said to me, "This plan put me back in touch with my money. I appreciate it more!"

It's very much about making sure you're conscious of where you're spending your money. It's not an issue if you love *Starbucks*, and that's what you meant to spend your money on. However, we often encounter situations where people have actually spent way more money in those categories than they have any idea about.

We find that even as people are just starting the process, they quickly become more aware and are already making different decisions.

Jonathan: Is unconscious spending linked to the internal tracking you talk about?

Wendy: That's the mental accounting I talked about: trying to remember everything that you've done. And yes, it is unconscious spending that gets people into trouble because they forget what they've done and where they've spent their money. They talk themselves into certain things because they don't remember their past spending behavior in those categories. Some days, I'm lucky to remember what I had for breakfast, let alone where I spent my money.

By taking a cold, hard look at everything you have spent on your credit card and/or debit card over the course of a 90-day period, we're able to show you what you actually spend your money on.

We call this "putting up a mirror." It's not meant to be judgmental at all; it's just meant to bring all of the unconscious spending back into the consciousness. By switching to cash and using the *One Number Solution*™ spending comes back into focus.

The Solution

Jonathan: What's the solution?

Wendy: The solution is how we break it down. Once we've analyzed your spending and looked at all of your needs, wants, and what your goals are, we then boil it down to a single number that is your *One Number Solution*™—that weekly cash number. That's how we help you stay on track. You get the money out on the same day every week, whether you have money left from the week before or not. That allows you to monitor your spending and determine if you are still inside the fence.

Going to the grocery store and having to pull out five $20 bills and count them feels very different than just handing the cashier a piece of plastic. It's much more personal and much more tangible. It forces people to make decisions, and it also results in different decisions. So many people aren't making decisions. They're just doing things until it becomes too late.

Jonathan: That's where the unconscious spending comes in?

Wendy: Exactly. To be clear, this is not just a phenomenon for people who may be low-income. This is a phenomenon for people making hundreds of thousands of dollars a year as well.

Our theory is, "The bigger the shovel, the bigger the hole." It's not something that is strictly connected to socioeconomic class.

In fact, if you look at the debt levels in Canada in particular, the higher your education, the more likely you are to have greater debt.

Jonathan: That's interesting. Why is that? Is it because people have more to spend?

Wendy: There could be more availability of credit for them, depending on where they are in their lives. If you're a doctor, you'll get almost anything you want in terms of credit, just based on what you do.

Jonathan: Is there a way to go about this plan of yours while using credit cards, or does it strictly deal in cash?

Wendy: There is a methodology. We prefer people start with cash, even for 30 or 60 days as it is far better from an adjustment of behavior standpoint to use cash. As a plastic using society we have forgotten how much $400 buys.

After the initial cash phase, we have developed an app to help people transition. It's an easy way to track spending if you still want to get points or use your credit or debit cards for things.

It also works incredibly well with couples who are sharing the same number.

Jonathan: Can you explain the power of compound interest and how it is important in the context of your plan?

Wendy: I think anyone who's seen any kind of presentation on the power of compound interest finds it fascinating that if someone, at the age of 25, starts putting away $25 a week for 10 years, in 10 years they'd have to do double that to get the same amount of savings. It's the power of making interest on top of interest, a snowball effect, so you're making a lot of money on your investments or savings.

What's important about compound interest is younger people who are putting this kind of plan into place don't have to put a lot of money away to have a lot of money later in life. With a good cash flow plan, they can have a very positive effect.

Also, compound interest is important in that sometimes people forget that when they use credit cards and don't pay them off each month, they're allowing them to have the power of compound interest on their purchases.

This phenomenon is also why we often recommend saving *and* debt reduction at the same time.

I have a theory called "the price versus the cost". If I had a $100 meal at a very nice restaurant, and it was absolutely amazing, then it was worth every penny of the $100.

If I put that $100 on my credit card and don't pay it off for a period of time, I would be paying 20% interest on it and would have to add the interest on top of the $100 price of the meal. I should also add on the opportunity cost of what I could have done with the interest that I'm paying. Then I have to consider how much money I have to make before I pay the taxes to actually pay off that bill.

Once you start looking at that as the actual cost of the meal, it may not have been worth it.

If they leave it on for a year, and then if they could've invested that same $20 for 10 years at 6%, what would that have made you?

Another way to look at the price versus the cost is to consider these elements when it comes to purchasing a vehicle. The price of the car is the monthly payment. To compute the actual cost of the car, we have to add in the new tires we have to buy, the amount and number of services we pay for and other maintenance items. For example, your car payment might be $500 a month, but if you have to buy a new set of tires for $600 every year, the actual cost is $550 per month.

It is so important to look at the actual cost, not the price when we are considering our buying decisions.

Jonathan: How does one set oneself up for success?

Wendy: For the client, it's about being aware of what they're doing, knowing exactly how they're spending their money and where it is going, so they can make sure it's doing the things they want it to do.

The *One Number Solution* ™ is a system that doesn't require tracking. On cash day, the client withdraws their money and, as it is needed, they use it. If it's a big grocery week, they spend a little more of their cash. If getting a haircut, they grab only the money they need before going off to get the haircut.

If cash day is Saturday, the following Saturday they get more money. In some weeks they will spend more than the weekly number, and in other weeks they will spend less, but as they build buffers, it works itself out. It allows more flexibility because not every week or month is exactly the same in terms of what they need to spend.

Jonathan: "How to Spend Your Way to Financial Freedom" isn't just about spending, it's also about saving, correct?

Wendy: If saving is important to you, then we make sure that saving is part of how you're deploying your money.

When I say, "Spend your way to financial freedom," it's about knowing how much you can spend on the behavior-oriented items. For instance, grocery purchases can be affected by your mood, and how much you spend at a clothing store can be affected by your mood.

On the other hand, if you're having a bad day or a really good day, you don't necessarily say, "I think I'm going to put an extra payment on the mortgage today." Across the board, spending based on mood can get people into trouble. That's the kind of spending that we're really trying to help people get a handle on.

We know that they know how to spend for their mortgage, but if we can help them figure everything else out, then they know how much they can spend and still achieve their goals. They can do so without stress or anxiety.

Some people spend too much, but some people don't spend enough.

We talk a lot about living life for today versus living life for tomorrow. This plan helps you figure out your today *and* your tomorrow.

We worry about people who don't spend today and are saving it all for tomorrow because tomorrow might never come. Conversely, if they are spending all their money on living well today, tomorrow might not be so fun when it arrives. So it's about finding that fine line…for different people, that line is different.

Many traditional financial plans help you save for tomorrow; they tell you to save this much but don't explain how to do that. A traditional plan might state, "To achieve your goals, save $1,000 a month." Where do you get that $1,000 a month? The "how" is missing. The *One Number Solution*™ is the how.

Jonathan: Do the spenders go into shock when they see the "how"?

Wendy: We definitely try to avoid that. I'd say there's some art and some science in how we put the plan together.

There are standard formulas that I use as a starting point. Then I evaluate: I take a look at the number my formula has come up with, and I compare it to the reality data. Sometimes, based on my formulas, a person should really be spending 25% of what they've been spending every month on those categories we mentioned.

That situation is like someone being on the worst diet ever. It's so extreme that they can't sustain it and when they go off of it, they're going to binge, and it's going to be bad.

We look at our number as our starting point. Then we look at what their life is like and what is realistically attainable. To use the diet analogy again, we try to get them on a lifestyle diet that is achievable and manageable while still getting them ahead.

We propose plans which are sustainable and which allow people to achieve their goals realistically. If they went to 25%, would they reach their goals faster? Absolutely, but we have to be more realistic about what they are going to be able to do.

It's a little bit like when we look at their debt situation; maybe they have a little bit of student loan debt, a line of credit, and a few other things. The optimized way of paying off debt from a mathematical perspective would be to pay off the most expensive loan first and then go after the next most expensive one.

We tend to recommend people go after their smallest loan first. That gives them a win right away, encouraging them to continue that good behavior as opposed to doing something that might force them to wait a long time before they see results.

It's about how do we make it real for them, and how do we give them important wins? It's really behavioral finance more than strictly numbers or theory.

Jonathan: Wouldn't it be counterproductive to pay off the smallest rather than the largest loans?

Wendy: From an ideal point of view, absolutely, but we're trying to encourage a certain type of behavior.

Think about it from the dieting perspective. If you give somebody the win of losing three or four pounds in the first week, the likelihood they'll stay on the plan is much better than if they had gone about losing weight the perfect way and only lost one pound a week.

It is a bit counterintuitive, but it's all about giving the client a win, so they will keep doing it.

Jonathan: Essentially, it's a mental trick?

Wendy: Right. Again, money is not about math. We need to use systems that accommodate our human nature. Money is about the behaviors that have been ingrained in you from your parents since the time you were a child. Money is about how good or bad a day you had and how stressed out you are. It's about how many times you have purchased a full load of groceries one day and the next day ordered in because you had a really terrible day.

We've all done it. Again, it's not about what's right or wrong; it's about what is sustainable and how, as long as you stay within the parameters of the cash per week, everything works. You can do it, but it means that you won't necessarily have money to do everything right away. What's important to you?

Your One Number

Jonathan: If someone is interested in working with you to find their own *One Number*, how can they get in touch with you?

Wendy: They can go to:

www.BurnYourBudget.com

We're also setting up a reseller network, so there will be select advisors throughout Canada and the United States who can help them. Potential clients can find those people by going to:

www.CashFlowFreedomPlan.com.

Jonathan: Thank you, Wendy, for sharing this amazing information with us today.

Wendy: My pleasure.

Spend Your Way to Financial Freedom

Do you make good money but wonder if you could be doing a better job planning for your future and cringe anytime you hear the "B" (budget) word? Traditional budgeting is an outdated model which adds a layer of complexity to your life that confuses rather than simplifies planning for most of us. What if you had just *One Number* to keep track of so you can fully enjoy your life today without having to sacrifice your future?

That's where we come in. We help people just like you identify your *One Number Solution*™ so you can spend without the guilt and the nagging doubt that you should be doing more for your future.

Step 1: We work with you to understand what's important to you. What do you want to achieve? Do you want to travel? Do you want to buy a new house?

Step 2: We then layer what's important to you on top of where you are now. We take the time to understand what your current situation is and what you've been doing up to now.

Step 3: From there we analyze your unique situation to come up with your *One Number Solution*™; the plan shows you how you can achieve all your goals while also accommodating all of the risks that may come along the way. We automate everything as much as possible so that the only thing you have to worry about is spending your *One Number* each and every week.

If you'd like us to help, just visit:
www.BurnYourBudget.com and get started on finding your *One Number*.

www.ingramcontent.com/pod-product-compliance
Lightning Source LLC
Chambersburg PA
CBHW032256210326
41520CB00048B/4867